LINCOLN LIONS ROAR

NORTHERN LINCOLN ELEMENTARY

2022-2023

THANK YOU ALL FOR A WONDERFUL YEAR AT NORTHERN!!

Congratulations to all of our Grade 5 students! On behalf of the teachers and staff at Northern, we wish you all the best of luck in all of your future endeavors! May you always remember your memories of Northern; your good times with teachers and friends, your learning experiences, and how much you have grown as a learner! We are so proud of you and have enjoyed being part of your journey. Remember to always work hard, stay humble and be kind. You ARE Northern and we are so proud of each and every one of you!   We can not wait to hear of all of your future successes! Have a wonderful summer and best of luck as you enter LMS next year. You got this NLES Class of '23!

Sincerely,

Mrs. Denham, Mrs. St. Louis, Mrs. Moreau, and Mrs. Marzini

5

MUCCINO

OLIVER
BEAUCHEMIN

CONNOR
BROOKS

MELODY
CLUNE

AMAYAH
CORREIA

ROWYNN
CUTHILL

MADISON
ELLITHORPE

GRACE
EVANS

SCARLETT
FASANO

5

MUCCINO

EVAN
FERNANDES-TELLA

GABRIEL
GARZA

SIRIVALLI
GUDURI

TAYLOR
HARBOIS

VICTOR
HIRALDO

MITCHELL
MURPHY

LUIS
PEREZ

AAVIYANA
PETTIJOHN

CASSIE
REI

5

MUCCINO

RAMON
SALCEDO

CECILIA
SULLIVAN

CARRIE
TASKIN

LEVI
TREK

JAYDEN
VOISINE

SHEAMUS
O'CONNELL

JAXON
KURAS

Connor Brooks

Connor,
Congratulations finishing Elementary school! We are so proud of you! You are growing into such a smart, kind and hilarious young man. Continue to work hard, be kind and be yourself! Magic is believing in yourself, if you can do that, you can make anything happen. Can't wait to see what you achieve next!

Love You!
Mom, Dad and Ryan

Oliver Beauchemin

Oliver,
We are SO proud of
you and can't wait
to see where your
journey takes you.
Love,
Mom and Dad

Grace Evans

Congratulations on completing
elementary school. You overcame
many obstacles and we are so
proud of all your accomplishments. We are beyond
blessed to have such a smart, talented, kind, funny,
and beautiful daughter. We love you to infinity and

beyond and are excited
to see you grow and move
on to middle school. Keep
being the best you, you
can be!

Love-
Mom, Dad and Jaxson
xoxo

Sheamus O'Connell

Sheamus,

We are so proud of you the smart, funny and kind young man you've become. We can't wait to see what you will do next- middle school here you come!

Love,

Dad, Mom, Katherine, Claire and Elizabeth

Cecilia Sullivan

Cece,

We are beyond proud of you for all that you have accomplished and cannot wait to see what lies ahead. Remember to stay true to yourself, dream big, keep working hard and always be kind, for these are the ingredients to success. We love you the most!!

xoxo,
Mom and Dad

"Keep moving forward, opening new doors, and doing new things... your curiosity will lead you down the path of success." - Walt Disney

Carrie Taskin

5

RHAULT

CAMERON
AHMAD

ZOYA
AHMED

KAYLIANNA
BAILLIE

LACEY
BLICKER

TYE
BRUYERE

EMILY
CROTEAU

ALEX
DEMARCO

SKYLAR
DOULL

5

RHAULT

JAXEN
EZOVSKI

QUINN
FERSCHKE

KINSLEY
GIGUER

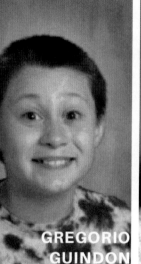

LILY
GILSON

GREGORIO
GUINDON

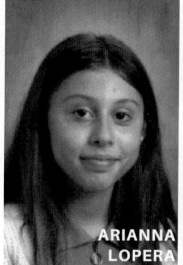

ARIANNA
LOPERA

CADEN
MCCOY

EMERSON
PEDROZA BOCHE

ARYEL REVERDES-
BAPTISTA

5

RHAULT

ELLA
SANTORO

SAMUEL
SANTOS

SOPHIE
TASKIN

BLAKE
VARGAS-BUCKLEY

SOPHIE
VITALE

BENJAMIN
ZAHLANY

ELOA
ZEFERINO

PICTURE NOT PROVIDED
Malikye Foster

Lily Gilson

Lily,
You have created your own path. We are so proud of the funny, creative and caring person that you have become. Can't wait to see what you do in middle school!
Love,
Mom and Dad

Be who you are....those who mind don't matter and those who matter don't mind. -Dr. Seuss

5

ROCK

ZAKARIA
ALI

LILLY
CARROLL

MADISON
CLARK

KYLEE
COSTA

AUSTEN
DUFF

LAYLA
GARRAHAN

AVA
GERUSO

ROCK

BRAYDEN JOHNSON

CHRISTIAN LOPES

KENZIE MELO

TIGRAN MNATSAKANIAN

MAKENZIE PARIS

AUBRY PERRICO

XAVIER RENE

GREGORY RIVERA

AMANDA-KARIS SARPONG

5

ROCK

MICHAEL THIBAULT

KENNEDY WRIGHT

Madison Clark

Maddie,
Congratulations!
We are so proud of you and all your many accomplishments! Look at how far you have come! You are growing into such an amazing young lady and we are so excited to watch you do BIG things in middle school. Go get 'em!

"Working hard is important, but there's something that matters even more... believing in yourself." – Harry Potter

We love you!
Morgan, Momma and Dad

Ava Geruso

You are so bright and talented and know you will succeed in anything you do. We are so proud of you and can't wait to see the wonderful things you do in middle school and beyond.

Love always,
Mom & Dad

Cameron Ahmad

Dear Cam,
Congratulations on finishing elementary school! We are so proud of your accomplishments and can't wait to see what your future holds!

Oh, the places you'll go!

With lots of love,
Your Mom and Dad

Amanda-Karis Sarpong

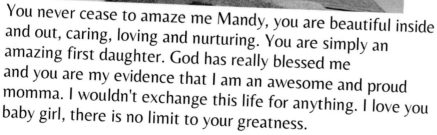

You never cease to amaze me Mandy, you are beautiful inside and out, caring, loving and nurturing. You are simply an amazing first daughter. God has really blessed me and you are my evidence that I am an awesome and proud momma. I wouldn't exchange this life for anything. I love you baby girl, there is no limit to your greatness.

Congratulations on Moving up to Middle School! You are going to be great and looking forward to all your accomplishments this new phase brings you.

Love you

Oliver
Beauchemin

Connor
Brooks

Melody
Clune

Rowynn
Cuthill

Madison
Ellithorpe

Grace
Evans

Scarlett
Fasano

Evan
Fernandes -
Tella

Sirivalli
Guduri

Cecilia
Sullivan

Carrie
Taskin

Jayden
Voisinet

Cameron
Ahmad

Zoya
Ahmed

Emily
Croteau

Alex
DeMarco

Skylar
Doull

Jaxen
Ezovski

Quinn
Ferschke

Lily
Gilson

Caden
McCoy

Aryel Reverdes
- Baptista

Ella
Santoro

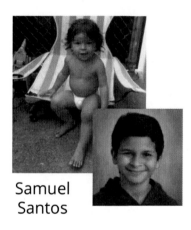

Samuel
Santos

Sophie
Taskin

Blake Vargas
- Buckley

Benjamin
Zahlany

Zakaria
Alil

Madison
Clark

Ava
Geruso

Brayden
Johnson

Christian
Lopes

Kenzie
Melo

Tigran
Mnatsakanian

Makenzie
Paris

Xavier
Rene

Gregory
Rivera

Amanda-Karis
Sarpong

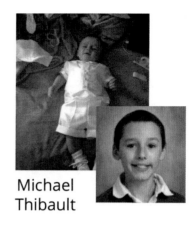

Michael
Thibault

Kennedy
Wright

Levi
Trek

Sheamus
O'Connell

Matthew
Daniel

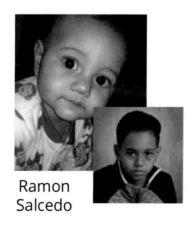

Ramon
Salcedo

Layla
Garrahan

Arianna
Lopera

Jaxon
Kuras

Lacey
Blicker

4

GOULIS

BENJAMIN
BEHLKE

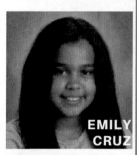
JAXSON
CARROLL

EMILY
CRUZ

ADELYNN
DESIMONE

JASMINE
FORTUNE

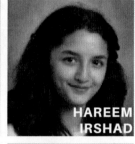
HAREEM
IRSHAD

AMELIA
LAFORGE

EMMA
LANDRY

ELIZABETH
LEWIS

MIA
MARCHAND

ARIANNA
MCGOWAN

CAMERON
MCKIERNAN

JONTEL
MIRANDA

LAYLA
MOREAU

CAMERON
PALIN

BRIDGET
PEDRO

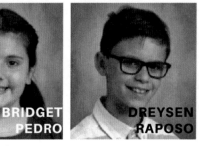
DREYSEN
RAPOSO

LIE
REYNOLDS

SYEDA
SAJJAD

4

DAMIAN SANTORO

ATTALIA-EVELYN SARPONG

RYAN TEED

JEREMIAS VILLAR JIMENEZ

PICTURE NOT PROVIDED
Preston Dean

GOULIS

4

HADDAD

BLAKE
ALEXANDER

BRANDON
BARNES

VICTORIA
BARNES

ANNABEL
CARDONA

LILYJOU
DAIGNAULT

MADELYN
DAIGNAULT

MARLIE
DANIELS

SHANE
DURAND

TONY
ELIAS

OWEN
HODGDON

LEO
JAMES

JAYSON
KAPP-CHALK

LUCIANO
MACHADO

LILY
MCGURN

CECILIA
NOBLE

ALEXANDRA
RIVERA

JOANNA
SCARBOROUGH

ANGELIA
VO

JAYACE
WELCH

PICTURE NOT PROVIDED
Andre Medeiros-Duarte, Brayden Santos,
Rishik Syam, and Mikayla White

4

SILVESTRI

MAKAI BARKER

LAILAH CAJOUX

ATHENA CINTRON

SADIE CLARKE

MYLAH DAVIES-CALHOUN

ALEAH FERNANDEZ

JACOB GORMAN

NATALIA GUEVAREZ

SOFIA HEREDIA

TRISTON HOULE

JORDAN IACOBUCCI

JOURNEY JOLY

DYLAN LEWIS

PEYTON MARTINEZ

HYFA MARYAM

JENNIFER MORRIS

BENJAMIN PINA

ADAM PLACEO

MOLLY RIEL

4

GRAYSON RICCHIO

SOPHIA SANTIAGO

MATTHEW V

ZARA WINT

PICTURE NOT PROVIDED
Emma Kalflan, and River McGrath-Caffrey

PAISLEY ZINNI

SILVESTRI

OLIVIA
ARRUDA

SALMA
BAKKARI

EDWARD
BAKLEH

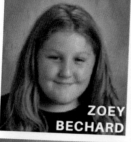
ZOEY
BECHARD

KUSHAAL
BUKKE

AARON
GOITIA

SEICHALYZ
GOMES TORRES

MARSHALL
GRASSO

LILLY
HADUCK-CURRY

LIAM
HOPKINS

BRIELLE
LAFERRIERE

DANIEL
LANERES

KHLOE
LONGPRE

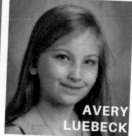
AVERY
LUEBECK

BAYLEE
MIRANDA

LEAH
MOORE

MASON
PLANTE

RONAN
QUISH

ARIELLA
RENTERIA

3

AMARA
RIVERA-HAROLD

GARRETT
SULLIVAN

KIYAN
THREATS

HANNAH
VO

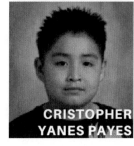

CRISTOPHER
YANES PAYES

PICTURE NOT PROVIDED
Olivier Joseph, and Finnlan Lyon

BERNIER

PROVOST

3

HARRISON
ARGIRO

MILEY
BASSETT

RE
BEAUCHEMIN

AVA
BELLUCCI

BRYANT
BOULIS

NOAH
BROWN

ISAIAH
CHURCH

LOUIS
DACOSTA

MELEAH
DANIEL

BREANNA
EMMONS

EMMA
FURTADO

MIA
GARCIA GOMEZ

MELODI
HELENA

PIERCE
JOSEPH

KARLEA
LEBEL-ROSE

HUNTER
LOPES

MIA
MINICHIELLO

NOELLE
MORKUNAS

CHARLOTTE
PAYEUR

JUSTIN RUSSELL

SEAN SULLIVAN

ARIA WHITE

AVERY WRIGHT

PICTURE NOT PROVIDED
Jayleen Bedoya, Brayden Bello, Marshall Lepine, and Anush Puttagunta

PROVOST

SCHMIEDEKNECHT

③

MARIA ARAUJO
DOS SANTOS

HARRISON
AUCLAIR

ELI
BEGIN

SARAH
BERGERON

SHARBEL
BOUTROS

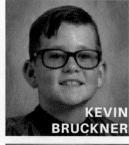
KEVIN
BRUCKNER

MORGAN
CLARK

AMAYA
DOIRE

BRYNLEE
DURAND

GEORGE
GHIZDAVU

ARIA
LANCTOT

BRADY
LAWSON

CHARLOTTE
LEWIS

MACKENZIE
MALOOD

KATHERINE
O'CONNELL

MYA
OAKLEY

JONSEL
ORTIZ

ABIGAIL
RENTERIA

CAMERON
RIEL

LIDIA RONCONE

JAKE RUSSO

AVERY SONG

AALIYAH WHITAKER

SCHMIEDEKNECHT

ANIYAH WOODS

JULIAN STUMBRAS

PICTURE NOT PROVIDED
Jackson Evans-Cooper, and
Osiris Perdomo

2

ALLEN

LUCA ADAM

AMEYA ARAVIND

CECILIA CHELO

GAVIN GERMAIN

JAMESON GOODE

KEANNA KENDALL

GEORGE KENYON

AUDREY LAFORGE

MASON MARTY

SARAH MASOOD

BRADY MEDEIROS

TAYLOR MONTMINY

ALYSSA MOREAU

GAVIN OCAMPO

COLIN RIEL

KAYSON RONDEAU

JOSEPH SILVA

JEREMIAH VACHON

BENJAMIN VOLPE

PICTURE NOT PROVIDED
Hailie Fedorak, Hazel Fontaine, and
Gianna White

2

DANIELS

BROOKE BOUTAN

BRA~~~~YN BROWN

GIANNI CALZO

~~CY T~~KIN

YENA CUI

ELYN FREEMAN

HAILEY GIGUERE

BENJAMIN HARRINGTON

WILLIAM JALETTE

AIDEN JAROSCH

MIA JOHNSON

MAXWELL LAING

JUDE LYON

JAYCEON MONTEIRO

AKASHA PARMENTER

CAROLINE RICHARDS

ARCHER ROCCHIO

JASE ROMERO

CONNOR SULLIVAN

DANIELS

2

MALENFANT

ELIANNA ARCAND

ZACHARY BETTENCOURT

VINCENT BONGIORNO

MALAKHI BROWN WHALEN

DAYSIA DOMENECH

JUSTIN EZOVSKI

BAILEY FARRELL

SAWYER GONCALVES

GWENYTH MATSON

GIOVANNI NOLAN

HENRY POZZUOLI

CARLEY REI

AVERY REYNOLDS

NAOMI SANTIAGO

CHLOE SCIACCA

NORA SIDDIQUI

NATHAN TEED

OLIVIA VIERRA

SHALEY VYAS

PICTURE NOT PROVIDED
Analisia Duquet, Heloisa Leite, and Tyler Ruscher

1

AUBIN

CONNOR BOULIS

ADRIANNA DAVIDSON

DORA DIAZ MUNIZ

LANDON DOIRE

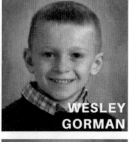
WESLEY GORMAN

RAFAEL GUEVAREZ

DECLAN HARRIMAN

MALANI OLIVEIRA

RIAAN PATEL

DOMINIC PORTUOBDO

KYLE RIVERA

DERICK SHORTS

OLIVIA SPANN

CHLOE TASKIN

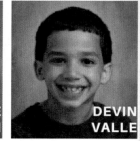
DEVIN VALLE

ANTONIO WILLIAMS

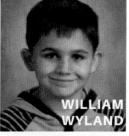
WILLIAM WYLAND

PICTURE NOT PROVIDED
Julian Bonne-Annee, Ghanishka Guduri, Loveanna Machado, and Hunter Pruneau

1

CASALI

KOLTON BEGIN

ASPEN BLAIS

KEYNER BRAVO - VALENTINE, JR

MOSHIKA BUKKE

DANNY CARRERA

JARELIS CASTRO

ABIGAIL DECOSTA

CARSON FONTAINE

JUDITH JIMENEZ

REAGAN LANERES

JAMESON LEINER

ISABELLA MARIANI

KARMELA MCNAMARA

JAMILAH NDIAYE

ELHADJI NDOYE

CLAIRE O'CONNELL

LIAM TRIVINO MONTANO

JUDAH WILKINSON

JEREMY ZIOBROWSKI

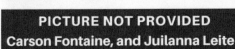

PICTURE NOT PROVIDED
Carson Fontaine, and Juilanna Leite

RODRIGUES

1

WILLIAM
AHLVIN

ZAYN
AHMED

MICHAEL
BENNETT

JAMES
BETTENCOURT

ANGELINA
BOUTROS

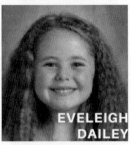
EVELEIGH
DAILEY

AUTUMN
FORTUNE

ADRIANA
GOMES

NATHAN
GRASSO

SOLOMON
HUDSON

SKYLAH
JOHNSON

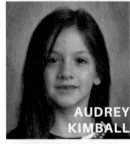
AUDREY
KIMBALL

DAISY
KING

MIA
LUCCHESI

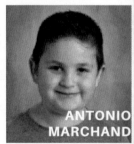
ANTONIO
MARCHAND

JEFFREY
KIMBALL

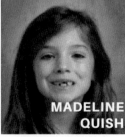
MADELINE
QUISH

GREGORY
RICHARD

ETHAN
VO

PICTURE NOT PROVIDED
Bentley Fedorak, and Enrique Lopez

ROWLAND

1

OKUNOLA
AINA

LILIANA
ARGIRO

OPHELIA
CROCE

JOVANI
DEPINA

CAMERON
DOIRE

ZAHRA
ELIAS

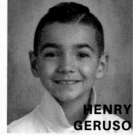
HENRY
GERUSO

SLATER
HOYLE

PAXTON
LOPES

TYLER
MEJIA

ZOEY
MELENDEZ

DANIEL
MORADEL

AMINATA
NDIAYE

ELLE
PEARSON

EVANGELINE
QUEDEVEZ

ARIANA
RAPOSO

NICO
SALVADORE

PICTURE NOT PROVIDED
Hayden Hazard, Wyatt Pruneau, and
Vallerieh Rodriguez-Concepcion

ANDREWS

BENJAMIN
BEDARD

OLIVIA
BELLUCCI

RYAN CAWLEY-
PANONE

MICHAEL
CHELO

ELIZABETH
CHURCH

JACOB
CLOSSON

WILLOW
COTE

JAIEL
CRUZ

SIRENA
DAVIDSON

KYLER GOMES
RODRIGUES

MAEVE
GUGEL

LONDON
JOHNSON

ELIJAH
LARA

ALANAH
LOPEZ

CASPER
MASANZ

JAXSON
MEDEIROS

PATRICK
MERRILL

GIULIANA
PORTUONDO

GEMMA
RONDONE

GIULIA
RONCONE

EMMA
SCIACCA

PICTURE NOT PROVIDED
Meadow Dean, Grayson Lefebvre, Mishal
Masood, and Emorie Parent

ANDREWS

BROCHU

GABRIEL
BAIRD

ADELA
BURLEY

ARIEL
CARDONA

HOLDEN
CARON

ALEXA
CARVALHO

JUSTIN
CUI

ZELIE
DWELLY

AUBREY
FALLS

KIARA
FIGUEROA

ADONNIS
HOLMES

GRANT
IRVINE

ISAIAS
LOPES

CARMEN
OQUENDO

THOMAS
PERRON

MAYLAMAY
RAMOS

YARELIS
RENTERIA

CHARLOTTE
SCIACCA

MICHAEL
SJODAHL

RUBY
SOARES

RENEE VIERRA

BROOKLYN ZINNI

PICTURE NOT PROVIDED
Eli Kalflan, and Allyanna Whitaker

BROCHU

PK

COOKE

MARCUS BARROS

LANCE BONCI

AVIANA CAMBIO

SAMI KARALIS

GUINEVERE BLODGETT

ABIGAIL PLACIDO

BROOKELYN CARO

LUCAS CLIFT

AALIYAH COELHO

CARTER DESAUTEL

JASMINE FENNER

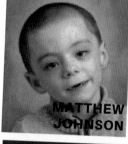
MATTHEW JOHNSON

ARIA ROSE

DANIEL VIRGULAK

PICTURE NOT PROVIDED
Milena Kapp, Jaiden Melo, Liam Santos, Shrihaan Sharaf, and Kai-Alexander Pena

PK

DANIELS

MATEO LEBLUE

ALYSON CABRAL

LILLIAN CARUSO

MYLES DAVIS

AUSTIN DIEBOLD

JAMESON FENNER

VIOLET HORTON

KENDALL MARTIN

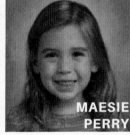
MAESIE PERRY

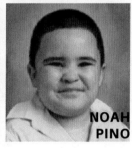
NOAH PINO

KARI SISSON

ISABELLA TORREJON DUMAIS

PICTURE NOT PROVIDED
Adam Marsh, Yusra Haruni, and Eeshwari Vanukuri

PK

ELEMO

VERNON KIMBALL

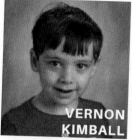
DAVID FIELDING

ROCCO FOSTER

PHILIP IGNACIO

HALIMA NDOYE

OLUKOREDE AINA

GIOVANNA CHRISTIANSON

JUDE GUGEL

BENSON LOPES

MAYA LUIS

NOLAN O'BRIEN

PICTURE NOT PROVIDED
Raymond Herbermann, Hendrix LeBeau, John Bellows, Own Hill, Demari Northup-Richardson, and Joseph Taylor

PK

HERRON

ROSITA BUNAY GUASCO

WILLIAM BAZINET

NATHALIE CASTRO

SANTIAGO HERRERA YANES

BROOK MORADEL

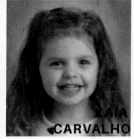
LAIA CARVALHO

SEBASTIAN FITZGIBBONS

SALVATORE PLAMONDON

COLTON SOULIERE

PICTURE NOT PROVIDED
Vivian Horton, Mason Arminio, Jasper Gao, Anvay Puttagunta, and Cameron Havandjian-Pattock

PK

KING

LUCAS
BARROS

RYAN
BELLUCCI

CLAIRE
DESILETS

HARLEY
ROGERS

LUCCA
ROCHE

NASH
WALKER

AMBER
BRODEUR

AUBREE
BROUILLARD

SPENCER
GONCALVES

AMELIANA
HERNANDEZ

CYDNEY
JACOBS

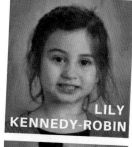
LILY
KENNEDY-ROBIN

ALICIA
LOPEZ

CHARLOTTE
MORRIS

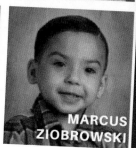
MARCUS
ZIOBROWSKI

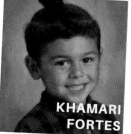
KHAMARI
FORTES

PICTURE NOT PROVIDED
Jacob Fletcher, Paisley Wood, and Jack
Sousa

PK

SMITH

ABDOU PAYE

JAMES IANNUZZI

ELLIANA JONES

NOBLE PARMENTER

CRUZ DURE

YEIDE LUG

SAMIRA BAKKARI

ALEXANDRA CARNEAU

NOAH GERMAIN

DEAN PEARSON

SAWYER SMITH

MARGARET SWEENEY

SOFIA TAYLOR

LUKE MATSON

PICTURE NOT PROVIDED

Eric Abercrombie, Gwyneth Gray, Oliver DiFilippo, Greyson Leary, Greyson Brunelle, Gianna DeMelo. Violette Krasko, and Jackson Abdirkin-Song

A DAY IN THE CLASSROOM

FIELD TRIPS

WALK FOR HEALTHY HEARTS

GLOW YOGA

UNITED SKATES OF AMERICA

SPRING
ART SHOW

FAMILY FITNESS

HALLOWEEN
BINGO

CERAMICS

NIGHT

HOLIDAY
BAZZAR

NORTHERN'S GUESTS

Alyson Cabral

Alyson Jaymes - We are so proud of you! You have come so far in pre-K. You amaze us every day. We cannot wait to see what you can accomplish next year!

XOXO Mama, Daddy, & Na-Na (and Link & Leia) <3

Brady Lawson

Brady,
Congratulations on a great year! We are so proud of you and of how hard working and determined you are! Shoot for the stars!

We love you!!

Mom and Dad

Casper Masanz

Congrats to our student of the month!

We love you Casper!

Santiago Herrera Yanes

If you Dream it, you can do it!

Aubrey Falls

You are so brave, outspoken, intelligent and silly. We can't wait to see you blossom into the person you're meant to be.

We will always be on your team.

With all our love,
Mommy & Daddy

Gregory Richard

Gregory,
Congratulations on completing 1st Grade! We are so proud of the son, brother, and friend that you are.

Dream big dreams!

Love,
Mom, Dad, Liam, and Lucas

Jayace Welch

Congratulations Jayace !
I am so proud of you. Believe in yourself always and never give up on your dreams. We love you forever and ever!

Love,
Mom and Brylen

Blake Alexander

Blake Elizabeth,
I am so proud of you and all of your achievements! Keep working hard and always follow your dreams. Never stop believing in yourself!

Love,
Dad

Jovani Depina

SONIC.... I mean JOVANI,
I am so proud of you!
You are a Talented boy, a hard
worker, and most importantly
a loving and caring person.
It is a joy to be your Mother!
Remember I am always here
for you!

Love you!
Mom

Jojo,
We are so proud of the little
man you are becoming.
We cannot wait to see how
far you will go in life, and see
all that you will accomplish!

"An adventure is no fun if it's
easy." -Sonic

Love,
Titi lily, Tio Chucky, Lena,
and Eli

Mason Plante

The MORE that you READ,
the more THINGS you will KNOW.
The MORE you LEARN,
the more PLACES you'll GO!

~Dr. Seuss

Love,
Mom & Dad

Matthew & Benjamin Volpe

MJ & Benjamin,
Another awesome year in the books as
you finish fourth and second grades.
You tried a lot of new things this year:
basketball, flag football, and lacrosse,
how fun! Mj became an avid football
fan (alongside his favorite football
buddy, Pepe) and Benjamin found his
groove in school, woohoo! Always be
kind and happy, just keep smiling! We
love you to the moon and back, no
matter what!

Love, Mom & Dad

Attalia-Evelyn Sarpong

Fierce Bold Brave is exactly who you are! You never cease to amaze me Talia.. You are such an incredible girl who is not afraid of anything. You make me proud and you are my proof that I am doing something right as a mother. You are great and highly favored. There is no limit to your greatness. You will forever be my silly goofy baby girl. 5th grade is going to be great!

Love you always and forever~ momma and sissy

Bryant and Connor Boulis

Bryant and Connor,

Congratulations on an amazing school year! We are so proud of your accomplishments in the classroom and on the ice!

We love you so much!!!

xoxo
Mom and Dad

Justin Russell

Jay,

I love you so much! Work hard, chase your dreams, and remember that I'm always here for you.

Love you more,
Mom

AUTOGRAPHS

AUTOGRAPHS

AUTOGRAPHS

AUTOGRAPHS

Northern Lincoln Elementary 2022-2023 yearbook
Copyright © 2023 Northern Lincoln Elementary School
Produced and printed by Stillwater River Publications.
All rights reserved. Written and produced in the United States of America.
ISBN: 978-1-960505-30-9